Carrington

Paintings, Drawings and Decorations

Noel Carrington

CARRINGTON

Paintings, Drawings and Decorations

Foreword by Sir John Rothenstein

Thames and Hudson

© Noel Carrington 1978
Foreword © Sir John Rothenstein 1978
First published by Oxford Polytechnic Press 1978
This revised edition first published in the USA by
Thames and Hudson Inc, 1980

Library of Congress
Catalog card number 79-3717

Printed and bound in Great Britain

Contents

List of Plates

Foreword

In spite of the substantial volume of her own writing published in David Garnett's edition of her *Letters and Diaries* in 1970 and an earlier account of her life with Lytton Strachey by Michael Holroyd, Carrington remains an elusive figure, especially as an artist. Indeed until the *Letters of Mark Gertler* were published in 1965 the artist Carrington had been virtually forgotten. Of her several creative occupations, painting and drawing were beyond comparison the most passionate, yet they remained almost unknown. During her life she exhibited very rarely and in her later years not at all. No exhibition of her work as a whole was held until 1970, thirty-eight years after her death.

In the London art world until recently the name 'Carrington' struck only a vaguely familiar note and that because of her strange relations with Lytton Strachey, Mark Gertler and others, but as a painter and draughtsman, it might well have been asked, 'What has she done?' During my long years as Director of the Tate I neither saw an example of her work nor heard allusions to it serious enough to make me attempt to see it. It was never mentioned by any Trustee at our meetings. I must confess therefore to a certain shame when I was invited (as one who had made a study of the art of her period) to

'The Feet-bathing Party'. Watercolour, 1919

9

Organ grinder. Pencil drawing, c.1914

contribute a few words by way of introduction to the present volume and was able to see examples of her original work as well as many reproductions.

Carrington's achievement is the more extraordinary in the light of the circumstances of her life. She died aged thirty-nine; apart from her three Slade years her closest friends were, with the notable exception of Gertler, literary rather than visual in their outlook. Thus she had few of those contacts with painters that would have satisfied her desire to study and discuss painting. It is true that throughout her life she remained friends with Augustus John and Henry Lamb, often visiting the Johns' home at Fryern, while Lamb was a regular visitor at Ham Spray, but her letters do not suggest that in either case there was much communication about painting. Her love affairs and friendships were complex and often distressing; much of her energy was devoted to a voluminous correspondence, with delightful illustrations. She also designed tiles, cut book plates, illustrated books for the Hogarth Press, painted inn signs, designed furniture and rooms for houses where she spent her later years. It is in fact testimony to her extraordinary and dedicated energy that in a life of this kind she should have found time to pursue and develop her rare talent for painting and drawing. Although rather less than fifty paintings were collected for the exhibition in 1970, her correspondence refers to many others which must unfortunately be regarded as lost. It seems that she was in the habit of overpainting a canvas when her work failed to fulfil her exacting standards. What remains, however, is sufficient to show what a considerable painter she was.

As painter and draughtsman she had one notable advantage. Her vision was linear; she was at her best when she was precise and this essentially linear vision had been ably nurtured during the three years (1910–13) she had spent at the Slade, not only by her teachers, Tonks and Steer, but by fellowship with Nevinson, the Spencer brothers, and Paul Nash, and, more important than any, Mark Gertler. Like her Slade contemporaries she was deeply influenced by the leading Post-Impressionists, and much of her subsequent artistic struggle resulted from the need to accommodate her highly personal vision to the Post-Impressionist examples.

She had another advantage, precocity. Had she not reached maturity so early, she might, again owing to her circumstances, have been prevented for all her innate talent from ever reaching it at all. This precocity is apparent in drawings she made while at the Slade, such as the self portrait of 1910 (Plate 30) and those of her brothers in 1910 and 1912 (Plates 32 and 33). None of them are markedly original; rather they are academic in the sense defined in the Oxford Dictionary, namely 'scholarly', traditional in the best sense of the term, and an ideal basis for the development of her personal way of seeing. This is apparent for instance in *Mrs Box* (1919, Plate 8), a masterly portrait of a Cornish farmer's wife, massive in form yet suffused with a tender insight conveyed by work-worn hands and the strong reticent face. In *Lady Strachey* (Plate 7), painted in the following year, and now in the National Portrait Gallery of Scotland, a similar massiveness of form offsets the face, alert, witty, dominant.

For all the stimulation they shared in visiting galleries and studying their favourite masters, Titian, El Greco, Cézanne and Matisse, the close association of Carrington with Gertler seems to have affected their work only in one respect. This was in portraiture. Their portraits could not have been more remote from 'face paintings'. The faces – naturally their subjects' most significant feature – were focal. Other features, particularly hands, received expressive treatment, for instance in the two already mentioned and in the *Lytton Strachey* (1916, Plate 4), which may be compared with Gertler's *The Artist's Mother* (1911) at the Tate or his

Two woodcuts. Illustrations for *Two Stories* by Leonard and Virginia Woolf, Hogarth Press, 1917

11

Kotelianski (1917). One other portrait of Carrington's can be singled out: that of her father (1915, Plate 1), for its tragic dignity.

Of her landscapes there are three, all of rare beauty, to which I would draw attention, as they show that her command of the panoramic was as sure as it was of the intimate. *Hills in Snow at Hurstbourne Tarrant* (1916, Plate 3), a watercolour view from her studio window, combines an exhilarating sense of space with the sharpest detail, everything of the austere leafless trees closely perceived. In *The Mill at Tidmarsh* (1918, Plate 5), the first of the two houses where she lived with Lytton Strachey, the love she had for it is apparent in every brush stroke and in the intimate perception of its every varied feature. The third is the *Farm at Watendlath*, Cumberland (1921, Plate 9).

In spite of an intense admiration for painters like El Greco and Matisse, who could hardly have been accused of traditional realism, Carrington had the courage to represent figures and landscapes as she saw them, and this at a time when the leading artists, in particular those of her own generation, were responding to, or imitating, rapidly changing 'movements'. Although her work reflects certain of the analytical preoccupations of the Cézanne-worshipping students of the Slade, she steadfastly remained a 'natural painter'. She had this at least in common with Constable, a devotion, unaffected by stylistic innovation or aesthetic theories, to her subject, preferably the familiar; and the greater the precision in both colour and form with which she represented it, the more impressive the result.

In her indifference to contemporary movements we can perhaps detect the influence of Gertler if we turn to his own letters. Thus in 1920, when he was immured at the Scotch sanatorium and she was consoling him with books and with reproductions, he writes: 'Oh those Goyas! How subtle, yet how vivid – Since Goya there's only been Cézanne, sometimes Renoir – no one else has that sense of paint. You know what I mean.' Gertler had visited Paris for the first time in 1920 and had thus been able to see in various collections what he had hitherto seen only in reproduction. He had reported to Carrington: 'About the more modern stuff I am not really at all sure: there is nothing that takes one's breath away like those giants.' When he came himself to be influenced by Picasso it was at a later stage in his career.

Her remoteness from the impulses which moved the most considerable of her contemporaries is at least one of the reasons why she has been the most neglected serious painter of her time.

JOHN ROTHENSTEIN
1976

But then I never said I was an animal artist

Page of a letter from Carrington to John Nash, c. 1912. (Reproduced by courtesy of the Trustees of the John Nash estate.) She was working on murals for Nash at this time

13

Samuel and Charlotte Carrington and their
second son Teddy. Pencil drawing, c.1910

Making of an Artist

1 Home

Dora Carrington, fourth child in a family of five, was born at
Hereford in 1893. Her father, Samuel Carrington, son of a
Liverpool merchant, had gone to India as a young man in
1857, the year of the Mutiny, to build railways for the East
India Company. He did not retire until he was in his fifties and
his letters to his parents over these many years have survived.
They give a picture of a God-fearing man, devoted to his
parents and a kind master to the Indians who worked under
his charge. By the time he retired to England, after travelling
through much of the East and in America, both his two sisters
had long been married, each with a family of a dozen; so that
his many nieces and nephews were already raising families in
their turn. One of these nieces, Ethel, had married Frank
Houghton, who had died in a yachting accident leaving her five
children to bring up. Her sister-in-law, Charlotte Houghton,
was thus brought into the Carrington circle and was acting as
help or governess to the Houghton children when Samuel
returned to England for good.

    He had saved enough during his railway-building career to
have a reasonable competence by Victorian standards and,
though rather deaf from overmuch dosing with quinine, was
still active and healthy, ready to satisfy his ambition to found

Samuel and Charlotte Carrington at their
marriage in 1888

15

a family. His choice fell on Charlotte Houghton, who was still in her thirties. They were married in 1888, settling at Hereford where one of his sisters was already established. During their married life, they migrated at regular intervals: to Berkhamsted, to Somerset, Devon, Hampshire, and then finally to Cheltenham where they had old family associations. Samuel Carrington's readiness to move house which, in those days, meant pantechnicons drawn across country by a traction engine, was partly to benefit his wife's rheumatism – which nonetheless was a match for all climates or soils – but I suspect it was also largely a habit acquired in India where 'striking camp' was in the nature of Anglo-Indian life. In 1903 he and his family moved to Bedford.

Bedford was then a county town of medium size with hardly any industries not connected with agriculture and market gardening. It was popular, however, for its cheap educational facilities which drew a large residential population of retired army officers and empire builders from overseas. The schools, both boys' and girls', were supported from the Harpur Trust

The market at Bedford. Pen and ink drawing, 1910

Pastel portrait of Carrington at the Slade
by Elsie McNaught, c.1911 (Reproduced by
courtesy of the Slade School of Art, London)

which drew its income from a considerable slice of Bloomsbury bequeathed by a successful Elizabethan merchant – Sir William Harpur and Dame Alice his wife – to his native town for the education of its children. At these schools, which Dora, her elder sister and three brothers all attended, more store was set on sport than on scholarship as conducive to character-building; and the majority of parents would not have had it otherwise. Bedford itself was still something of a religious stronghold where the various churches exercised great influence at all levels of society. The middle classes were loyal to the Church of England, whether High, Low or Broad in tone, and each sect had its favourite foreign mission; but the Non-Conformist chapels were more than able to hold their own in a town still proud of its most famous citizen, John Bunyan. All sects were united in one respect, the strict observance of the Sabbath, to the extent of banning not only sport or entertainment but such private pursuits as painting or playing music that was not hymnal in character.

Though only fifty miles from London by train Bedford might have been almost a thousand for all the cultural influence then exercised on it by the metropolis. An occasional concert by a touring pianist or a 'season' from Frank Benson's Shakespearean Repertory was almost the sum of it. Those with some claim to a feeling for art made an annual pilgrimage to the Royal Academy's Summer Exhibition. Our mother always brought back the illustrated catalogue, where the nudes could be guaranteed not to satisfy any sexual curiosity. In our living rooms, apart from my father's collection of Oriental curios, were several 'Old Masters' in ornate gilt frames, a reputed Velasquez self-portrait, a Murillo and others of the kind, and in our bedrooms were prints from Millais or Alma Tadema. In this respect a formal tribute at least was paid to Art, something I cannot recall observing in the homes of any of my friends. At no stage of her family life did Dora encounter

Dora Carrington, schoolgirl at Bedford, aged 15

opposition to her desire to be an artist. Her father liked to see his children using their hands and brains in leisure time. If Teddy could build model ships he was helped to get tools and timber, and if Dora loved to draw she was to have the materials. Her mother claimed that the talent came from her side, since she had studied at Lambeth Art School at some stage, and was proud to show her younger daughter's work to her 'second Thursday in the month' tea parties. In fact, Dora was the only one of the five to be excused 'practice', the name by which music study of some kind was known. It was just as well, as all of us were more or less tone deaf, and one absentee lightened the agony.

That Dora was something of a favourite with her father was undeniable, but for daughters to develop a special relationship with their fathers is not at all unusual. In her case it was accentuated because her mother was what children call a 'fusser'. Indefatigable in doing her duty as she saw it, she was, in spite of lameness, always on the move overseeing the servants or her children. And that preoccupation – so common with Victorians – 'What would the neighbours think?', was at the back of so much fussing. It is a motive that children easily see through and never respect. It became particularly oppressive during the frequent and prolonged visits of elderly relations. Samuel Carrington himself was unconventional in dress and in many other respects; his morality being based on his constant reading of the New Testament ('Love thy neighbour', 'Judge not that thou be not judged'), so that he pooh-poohed the suggestion that the vicar's wife would be shocked or that Aunt Mary was horrified. Such differences between parents were not voiced openly in front of the children, but they were sensed, and Dora built up a special image of her father's noble qualities. Some of this was derived from his old Anglo-Indian cronies who on rare occasions came to stop with us. They would spell out the respect with which he was held

Carrington the dutiful daughter, c. 1910

Carrington painting a portrait of her father, 1910

in India, by sahibs and natives alike; how he had fed a whole district from his own purse during a famine; of his generosity to friends in distress; all tales which we had never heard from himself. They were confirmed by an old Welsh doctor who lived with us for years. Of this Dr Roberts our father had said that a friend who had saved his life must never lack a home. It was natural enough for Dora, always an idealist, to feel a deep love for her father, and this surely renders it unnecessary to draw a psycho-analytical moral. At his death in 1919 at the age of eighty-seven, she wrote to Mark Gertler, who had lost his own father two years earlier, 'I loved my father for his rough big character, his rather rustic simplicity and the great way he lived inside himself and never altered his life to please the conventions or people of this century. He would have been exactly the same if he had lived under Elizabeth.'

While she had already begun to question the conventions of respectability and the many taboos which our mother wished to impose on us, she could hardly be termed a rebel during her life at school. Only drawing and natural history engaged her real interest, so that her general education was rather per-functory, but with two firsts in a school report she satisfied honour. She always had plenty of close friendships with girls and some with boys, and she joined her brothers willingly in games and expeditions on the river, though sometimes she exacted a penalty clause that we and our friends should sit as models.

2   The Slade

The art mistress of the High School persuaded the family that Dora must go to an art school. As there was no such institution at Bedford it was agreed that she should try for the Slade. Aged seventeen, she was planted at Byng House in Gordon

Square, a highly respectable hostel for students. None of her letters of that period survive, but I can well remember that even after one term she returned a very changed young person. Her opinions on art deflated all our previous conceptions; those revered elders, Lord Leighton, Alma Tadema, Herkomer and company were brushed aside as fit only for the dustbin. Who were we to look to, then? Why Sickert, Steer, John, McEvoy: names unknown to Bedford, and even these were not to be mentioned in the same breath as Cézanne. It was rather humiliating for my poor mother, who now hardly dared to talk on the subject for fear of mispronouncing these strange names.

I recall another shock I received at this time. Though a couple of years younger, I had a schoolboy's sense of mental superiority over any girl, and here she was reading books beyond my ken: Tolstoy, *Tristram Shandy*, Mary Wollstonecraft, and Romain Rolland. I was called on to contribute occasionally with facts and dates or with the loan of my textbooks on English literature or history. It was the beginning of her long odyssey in self-education. Of this I shall have more to say later.

As far as art was concerned Tonks had already knocked out of her all fanciful and careless nonsense. Accurate draughtsmanship was what now mattered. Her old compositions that had once been shown around with pride, were now torn up or hidden. All of us in turn were bribed to pose. My father, being partially paralysed, was a willing if captive sitter. Even my school friends succumbed to her wiles and sat patiently for their portraits. Temporarily painting was abandoned, discouraged I think until draughtsmanship was perfected. Such was the regime at the Slade of Tonks and Brown. We could savour some of its mental attitudes when her student friends came to stay, as they often did, though only the women in Bedford days. All were entirely serious about their art and their

Student at the Slade, 1911. With Carrington are Barbara Hiles (Bagenal) and Brett (Hon. Dorothy Brett, later disciple of D. H. Lawrence)

Off to Slade picnic by taxi 1912: Carrington on top.

intention to be the equal of men. They were to be addressed by their surnames and thenceforward 'Dora' was dropped for 'Carrington' or shortened by her intimates to 'Cally'. I do not recall that they were active suffragettes, but their opinions seemed very advanced compared with anything that my family had been accustomed to hear. Certainly an early influence at this time on my sister was C. R. W. Nevinson, one of her early Slade friends, son of H. W. Nevinson the radical journalist. Was this the beginning of her later dislike for her feminine weakness and for the restrictions which custom then imposed upon women in making their careers and in ordering their own lives? It was almost certainly at the Nevinsons' house in Hampstead that she began to acquire the feeling that a woman's role in life must not be one of sub-servience. Her friend, 'Chips' Nevinson, was something of a loner, introspective and suspicious of society. He fastened on to Carrington as a sympathetic innocent who was worth coaching in the facts of life and art. He was backing her to work for a scholarship. His advice was sound enough, but he seems to have expected too much in return. In any case he was bitterly disillusioned when she preferred Mark Gertler to himself; he regarded Gertler as his own friend, and wanted to retain a special place with both. Gertler was having none of that and Carrington was forced to choose between them. It was Gertler who was to have most influence on her early career.

Among her other men friends at the Slade those whose talents she most admired were Paul Nash, Stanley Spencer, Edward Wadsworth, William Roberts and Clive Allinson. John Nash aroused her interest in wood engraving and in watercolour landscape. She was also meeting older men, Albert Rutherston, Henry Lamb and Augustus John, at cafés, parties and exhibitions, but they could not mean as much to her as Gertler, who was of much the same age and made her party to all his enthusiasms and despondencies. It also appealed to her sense of romance that he was a poor Jewish boy from the East End, was good-looking and witty, and like her was educating himself in art and poetry. How could she resist an appeal like this? 'I will tell you why I want you. I find it impossible to paint without some person at the back of my mind. I mean that since I got to know you, I thought of you [sic] with every stroke I do. Now I find that I want you to see all that I paint and I keep considering what you will think of my work.' Such pleas were renewed in every other letter. One can imagine many young women preferring the expression of admiration in other forms, but not I think a young idealist of nineteen as she was then.

Reading the correspondence of those years one has to ask whether Carrington herself derived as much support in her own development as an artist. In one of Gertler's first written proposals to her in 1912 he lists, after the fact that he was a

'Dante's Inferno'. Pen and wash drawing. Subject submitted for a Slade competition, 1911

23

very promising artist and likely to make a lot of money: 'I could help you with your art career. You would have absolute freedom and a nice studio of your own.' Because she already had doubts about the 'freedom' he promised, she did not consent. A fortnight later he writes to break off their friendship and says: 'I have suddenly begun to think you simply use me as a help to your work and for myself you don't care a scrap.' On this vital question of retaining her independence as an artist, let me quote from a letter she wrote Gertler in the Summer of 1917 when they had spent a week together at Cholesbury: 'I shall try later, if you still wish it, to spend more of my life with you. But I think it would be unfair if I promised to live with you, because I do not think I ever could. Yes, it is my work that comes between us. But I cannot put it out of my life because it is too much of my life now. If I had not my love of painting I should be a different person. I at any rate could not work at all if I lived with you every day.'

Quarrels and reconciliations went on for four or five years, but despite the tensions involved I would contend on the evidence that both benefited largely over the years from the relationship. It is true that he was so profoundly wrapped up in his own problems as an artist that these figure much more in the correspondence than hers. Also I suspect that he found it difficult to agree that women should aspire to be artists at all. Indeed when he wrote: 'You ought to learn something about cooking. I should always prefer my girl friends to be better cooks than artists', he was at least half serious.

For all that, her own letters show that she got from Gertler something that she needed, considering her excessive diffidence about her own talent. Thus in 1918: 'I like going away just to come back with a fresh eye on my past work. It fills me with disgust to see how little and how meaningless so much of my work has been. And you have no idea how inspiring it is to see paintings like yours.' To show that this was not flattering

Tile design – a Russian church

Gertler to compensate for having failed him in other ways, I will quote from a letter she wrote to me at the same time: 'He [Gertler] has done some frightfully good paintings lately, much better than those you saw in the summer [at Garsington]. He is so sincere, I am always more improved by him than anyone when I talk about painting to him.' Even as late as 1922 when her love affair with Gertler was a thing of the past she could tell Gerald Brenan: 'He [Gertler] has been to Paris lately and told me about the latest developments of Derain, Picasso and Matisse. I shall see Gertler often now because I find these discussions on technique and methods so important to one. One gets things straighter simply by arguing with opposition, things which have been confusing one's own ideas for months.' After all, there were difficulties where only a fellow artist could help. On one occasion she had written to him that she was 'stuck' with her painting 'when literally one can't think of anything to paint'. Gertler replied: 'I know that feeling well, that "blankness" you speak of is indeed terrible. Yet it is quite a healthy state. It usually means that one is growing, that one is dissatisfied to go on working in the same old way, that something new and more interesting must be found. In the meantime there is "The Blank" . . . In your letter you say that ideas come, but too vaguely to be of use. That is about the truest thing you ever said.'[1]

Apart from the help she derived from such discussions there was in their relationship something which for her reached far deeper. This, I am sure, was the revelation of the spiritual travail that an artist must go through even to the point of physical exhaustion. Such states of exaltation are constantly reflected in Gertler's letters to her, and it was this communion of spirit which drew her back to him after so many dissensions.

Her prolonged affair with Gertler has earned her many black marks from students of the period, chiefly on the grounds that she would neither give herself wholly to him nor give him up completely. Certainly, as one can gather from his letters, her professions of love but evasions in performance

Book plate

1. Mark Gertler, *Selected Letters*. Hart-Davis, 1965.

A Cockney picnic. Pen and ink drawing, c.1911

rendered him at times profoundly wretched. Nor did the advice of his friends, such as D. H. Lawrence, prove of much help: 'If you could really give yourself up in love, she would be much happier. You always want to dominate her, which is no good. One must learn to relinquish oneself, not to bother about oneself, but to love the other person. You hold too closely to yourself for her to be free to love you . . .' In Gertler's last letter to her, however, shortly before her death, he could tell her that after reading through her letters to him over the years: 'They certainly make the most interesting reading. It must have been the most extraordinary and painful time for both of us. But we were both very young and probably unsuited. And now it is nobody's fault. With love Mark.' I think he must have recalled that in the Slade and post-Slade days he had benefited too from their association, her enthusiasm for his work, their constant visits together to the galleries, their sharing of books and reproductions of art.

At Hurstbourne Tarrant with her dog, 1915

3   New Horizons

In 1914 Carrington's family had moved from Bedford to Hurstbourne Tarrant, a village in the Hampshire Downs near Andover. Ibthorpe House was a neat square Georgian farmhouse in a village that had been a favourite of William Cobbett on his rides and she never lost her passionate love of the hills and villages of this countryside. She converted a small barn into her studio where she was happy enough painting. Unfortunately too little of her work of this period has survived. One would like to have been able to see the painting she describes to Gertler in a letter of 1915: 'I will show you my landscapes sometime. I am very excited over the one I have just started. A big round spotted field like a basin covered with dark irregular bushes, and in the foreground an old man leading his thin horse on the end of a string.' A watercolour (Plate 3) is one of the few landscapes of this period that I have been able to trace.

She found her home life gloomy, with her father now crippled and her mother's circle of friends intolerant. 'Why was she not engaged on patriotic work in the midst of such a war, with three brothers at the front, etc.?' The young like to believe that never before was the 'generation gap' so wide as in their day. For Carrington it was perhaps accentuated by the age of her parents when they were married. She was twenty-four when in 1917 she described this incident at her Hurst-bourne home: 'awful row over these papers with my photo-graph about the Chelsea Matinée. Mother started the moment I got in the house. N. had brought the paper in of course with it. Mother sat and wept on Daddy's bed that night and he not understanding anything gave me a long sermon from the Old Testament. I went into Mrs Mack who gave me a long sermon too, saying she hoped I didn't know that awful man Augustus John. How even to be associated with his name for a brief moment would wreck any young girl's life. He had three wives! Well when you come home I'll take you there to tea with the Johns and you can judge for yourself what prattling old humbugs these people are . . .' She would have worked happily enough at Hurstbourne but I could understand it if she felt driven from time to time to escape to a borrowed and grubby studio in Soho or to teach the children of far-from-sympathetic rich families.

Nothing distressed our father more than family discords. Honouring one's parents was the Commandment most often quoted in those days to children. He must, however, have sensed that Dora would never be able to live in harmony with her mother, for he left her in his will a small legacy to assure her at least some independence. Even if it brought in something less than three pounds a week, it was an allowance on which a penurious artist would not at least starve.

It will not escape the reader that my sister and I did not see eye to eye on many social questions, but we remained very close friends and when I was in funds I was allowed to act as her banker. What impressed me when with her and her friends, like Gertler or Paul Nash, was their absolute dedication to their art as their life's work (as compared with the attitude of most of my friends) and also in her case her determination to remedy her lack of general culture. In return she plied me with periodicals like the *New Statesman* and *New Republic*, papers regarded at that time in France or in India as nothing less than 'Bolshie'. Many years later, reading Henry James's sketch of the young Isabel Archer in *Portrait of a Lady*, I was reminded of Carrington at the threshold of her career. 'The girl had a certain nobleness of imagination which rendered her a good many services and played her a great many tricks. She spent half her time in thinking of beauty and bravery and magnanimity: she had a fixed determination to regard the world as a place of brightness, of free expression, of irresistible

Book plate for Lytton Strachey, c.1916

Book plate, c.1917

29

action. She held it must be detestable to be afraid or ashamed.'

The War had inevitably broken up the community of artists which had formed amongst her Slade contemporaries. Some of the men, like Paul Nash, Stanley Spencer and Nevinson, were drawn into the Services as combatants or war artists, and several of the women had married. This latter step she regarded as a sad falling-off from a high ideal and the end of creative life for an artist. Of one of them she wrote to me: 'She is so absorbed in the babies that she becomes incapable of having rational conversation and her interest is entirely engrossed in the welfare of the infants. This may appeal to your "natural" state of mind. But to me it's degrading, as bad as ladies who can only talk of their pet dogs. Not for me at any rate.' We had recently spent my leave from France on a walking tour in the Highlands, during which she had done her best to convert me to her new creed of free association between the sexes. Her strong antipathy to the natural consequences of marriage hardened with the years. Neither at Tidmarsh nor Ham Spray, where she lived with Lytton Strachey, were children welcome, and this was not entirely because 'le petit peuple' would be a bore for Lytton's circle of intellectuals.

Carrington had met Strachey in 1915 at Asheham, the Woolfs' home in Sussex where a typical Bloomsbury weekend was in progress. The story goes that to punish him for giving her an unexpected embrace she stole into his bedroom with the intention of cutting off his beard. Thwarted by his opening his eyes to look at her, she forgot her purpose and fell hopelessly in love . . . At any rate from that time she certainly became charmed by his kindness, his learning and his humour and, while not intending to forsake Gertler, moved steadily away from him. Strachey was one of the central figures in the Cambridge-Bloomsbury élite. To the world at large and even to literature, he was still relatively unknown, his *Eminent*

Carrington in the garden, 1915

Victorians being still a year or two away. During the next two or three years, Carrington and Lytton were thrown more and more together either at Garsington Manor, Lady Ottoline Morrell's country refuge for pacifists, or in London. Considering the differences in their ages, their background and culture, not to mention his known homosexual nature, Lytton's response to her adoration puzzled his family and his close circle of friends. Nevertheless their love and companionship was to dominate the rest of Carrington's life.

It happened that Lytton was clearly much in need of a country retreat where he could work steadily at his books, instead of leading a rather peripatetic life between his family in Hampstead and various country houses. His brothers and Bloomsbury friends, including the businesslike Maynard Keynes, were ready to put up a fund to rent such a home, and Carrington was eager to slip into the role of housekeeper and companion. Indeed she willingly took on the burden of finding the house (mostly by bicycle), decorating it, scrounging the furniture and engaging a maid. This was Tidmarsh Mill, near Pangbourne. The mill was still working, but the Mill House, roomy if a bit dilapidated, was leased, mice and all, with a garden and orchard upstream.

For Carrington, Tidmarsh became an enchanted home, something beyond her dreams. There was Lytton to look after, cook for and generally spoil. She had time to paint and to garden. And there were weekends with endless good talk amongst his friends – the Strachey brothers and sisters, the Woolfs, Maynard Keynes, E. M. Forster, David Garnett or Desmond MacCarthy. There were occasions when I 'listened in' rather than participated in this talk; and it still seems in recollection to have been more brilliant and sustained than any I have heard since. This may be the moment to give my sister's own observations on Bloomsbury, writing in her last diary after Lytton's death. She says: 'I am not surprised,

At Garsington Manor: pose for a living statue in the garden. 1917

reading Lytton's old Cambridge letters, that their friendship for each other survived all "frenzies", even removes to other countries and old age . . . Their taste in humour and style is impeccable. After reading a great many letters I suddenly felt the quintessence of what had so often puzzled me. It was a marvellous combination of the highest intelligence and appreciation of literature with a lean humour and tremendous affection. They gave it backwards and forwards to each other like shuttlecocks, only the shuttlecocks multiplied as they flew in the air.'

It was, however, the quiet evenings with Lytton by the fire which came to mean most to her: when he read her Shakespeare or Keats, taught her French so that she could appreciate Voltaire or Racine, or read to her from his work in progress on the Victorians. She had already become ashamed of her ignorance of literature and history, which to her credit she never attempted to cover up by smart repartee. She set herself doggedly to amend her deficiencies. Thus in 1916 after a Christmas at Garsington when she described a set-to between Lytton, Clive Bell and Bertie Russell on one side and the Bishop of Oxford on the other, the subject being an American peace move, which was later followed by a play devised by Katherine Mansfield, she concluded with this postscript: 'I insist when you return that seriously you teach me English history and French. See? Because I am determined to be no longer so stupid and lacking in knowledge. I am going to start on my return to learn English history from Queen Elizabeth onwards.' She could hardly have found a more stimulating intellectual companion or a more sympathetic teacher than Lytton Strachey. Some years later, she writes to Gerald Brenan: 'The first summer I met Lytton was a good example of my extreme ignorance. Literally (and I was 22) I had only read *Wuthering Heights* and a few novels of Thomas Hardy and a few translations of Balzac, apart from my High School

Tidmarsh Mill as first discovered and reported in a letter to Lytton Strachey, 1917

Conversation piece at Garsington by Brett. Oil painting, c.1916. Amongst the figures are Lady Ottoline Morrell, Julian Morrell, Lytton Strachey, Aldous Huxley, Brett, Carrington, Katherine Mansfield, Middleton Murry and Mark Gertler (Reproduced by courtesy of the artist).

education at Bedford which was negative. You can imagine my agitation when Lytton read Donne and Shakespeare to me.' I do not imagine that a stunted education was particularly rare amongst art students. It was the impact of Bloomsbury that shattered her complacency.

These early years at Tidmarsh from 1917 to 1921 were the happiest of her life and also the most productive, for emotional fulfilment always stimulated her as an artist. One catches her mood in her letters, as this one to Lytton in the Autumn of 1920: 'The beauty of that walk made me long to be in the country again. To sit on the edge of the river and to paint those barns against the red stained woods . . . I love the smell of fallen leaves and the loveliness of the coloured trees and Tidmarsh so passionately, I cannot write what I feel.' Or this

33

Sign for Greyhound Inn, Tidmarsh

Sign for Roebuck Inn, 1921

to Gerald Brenan: 'Oh you have no idea how lovely Tidmarsh is this winter. I feel so moved by it. I would like to write a long descriptive essay to show future eyes what an amazing country England was in these years. I have been painting a little landscape from the top of the house of the village, the yellow haystacks and barns and the tall witch elms six times as high as any cottage.' Of this period several paintings have survived, both landscapes and portraits.

What she increasingly missed was the company of other artists. David Garnett has commented: 'It did not occur to Lytton Strachey or Ralph Partridge that her painting should be put first.' (Carrington married Ralph Partridge in 1921.) How much she really needed the company of other artists or critics whose opinion she respected comes out frequently in her letters. In 1917 she wrote to Gertler from Cornwall: 'I long to be back with you and Brett. There is a confession – but when I was at Charleston it was good to be with artists to talk about paintings and sometimes I feel strongly isolated having lost my companions.' Charleston meant Duncan Grant, Vanessa Bell, and probably Clive Bell too.

Though not lacking in courage she remained diffident about her own talent as an artist, and this diffidence was shown in her reluctance to exhibit in public. She had entered work once or twice for the New English Art Club or the London Group, though without much success, and later she could not be induced to exhibit at all. She was a severe critic of her own work and tended to judge by the highest standards. As early as 1915 she could write to Gertler: 'My work disappoints me terribly. I feel so good, so powerful before I start and then when it's finished I realise each time it is nothing but a failure.' Such cries of despair must be voiced by most artists at times. They recur again and again in her letters. 'I look at my favourite Piero della Francesca and then give up in despair at my amateurish painting. I feel glad I never sold any of my work and that my disgrace is known only to myself.' The last sentence reveals a strain of secrecy which ran deep in her nature. Something of this comes through in an entry made in her private diary in 1917 after completing her portrait of Lytton (Plate 4): 'Looking at your picture now tonight it looks wonderfully good and I am happy. But then I dread showing it. It's marvellous having it all myself. No agony of the soul. Is it vanity? No, because I don't care for what they say. I hate only the indecency of showing them what I have loved.'

Who amongst artists were the major influences affecting her outlook? As a student at the Slade, Augustus John, Ambrose McEvoy, Duncan Grant, and amongst her contemporaries, Gertler and John Nash. It was the latter who drew her towards watercolour at one period and to wood engraving. She seems, however, to have been unaffected by the trends of the twenties such as Vorticism or Cubism, reacting to nothing in fact later than the Impressionists and Post-Impressionists whom Roger Fry had introduced to Londoners in 1912. She shared with Gertler an enthusiasm for Cézanne, Renoir and Matisse, but it seems to have stopped short at the later Picasso or Braque. In a letter written about 1927 she says: 'I think except for a few French artists and perhaps two English there are no important *living* artists. Painting hasn't advanced: there are few inventors and original artists alive now. They reduce painting to the same culture as architecture and furniture, always reviving some style and trying to build up a mixture with dead brains. Matisse seems to me one of the most definitely original artists alive now. I think all this "culture" and group system is partly the reason for the awful paintings produced.' And two years later her fury is aroused by a show of French painters in London: 'I could write you a long letter on these modern French. They filled me with unspeakable rage. They are fifty times worse than other painters, English

Cook and cat, painted on blind window at Biddesden House, Wilts., for Brian Guinness (Lord Moyne), 1931

Glass painting of Iris Tree, c.1925 (Reproduced by courtesy of Ivor Moffatt)

Book plate for St. John Hutchinson, the lawyer, whose wife Mary was a cousin of the Stracheys

or German, because they are morally wicked, being charlatans, cheats, imitators . . . they produce hideous, vulgar pictures. I shall be interested to hear what Roger and Clive have to say on these modern monsters.'

Her love of the great schools of European painting was the real source of inspiration. 1919 was her first opportunity to travel and see what she had hitherto known only in reproduction. On a walking tour in Spain she was able to visit Madrid, Seville and Toledo. The Spanish School held her loyalty for the rest of her life. She writes to Gerald Brenan on her journey from his cottage in Andalusia in 1920: 'On Wednesday I shall see the Prado again. These pictures make me want to give up everything and become an artist entirely. The importance of their work seems above everything else. How El Greco sweated with agony over every picture. One feels he never attacked anything that was not as hard as granite to him.' Of the Italians, she wrote to Brenan in 1924: 'I came to a great many agitating conclusions at the Louvre this morning. A conflict always arises in reconciling my passion for the early Siennese or the very early Florentine with the amazing solidity of Titian and Giorgione. I tremble over the delicate beauty of those little panels, the naive simplicity of their designs and the colour they are, but then when I see Titian and El Greco their powerful intellectual designs make me stand still and I cannot turn back and neglect them.' She adds: 'When I am at the Louvre I suddenly feel so certain of myself. I feel there is nothing to prevent my painting my now fervent image of the nymph who turned into a stag so perfectly that it could be no disgrace. Then I have a picture of those guitar players that I have drawn in miniature.' This last phrase refers to drawings she had made at Brenan's mountain home in Andalusia.

Her long correspondence with Gerald Brenan shows that she found in him a more receptive and understanding critic concerning art than most of her friends except Gertler. The acknowledged pundit of her circle in matters of art was Roger Fry. Anyone who heard his lectures on the great winter exhibitions at the Royal Academy had to acknowledge his supreme gift as an interpreter. During the twenties his authority was unrivalled. Encouragement from him would have made a world of difference to Carrington's confidence. Thus in 1918 she wrote to Gertler: 'I do take such pride in you as it is. When I hear the good things Roger and Borenius say about your work, I swell with pride.' Fry had been helpful to Gertler on more than one occasion. It was unfortunate, therefore, considering the respect in which she held him, that Fry remained critical of her own work, as indeed he was of that of many of the younger English artists.

There is an amusing letter from Gertler which he wrote her in 1919 reporting a visit made by Derain to London when he was taken to an exhibition at the London Group: 'Without knowing the names of the exhibitors he picked out pictures by Roger Fry as being the best. And at a party he saw a picture by Carrington and thought it excellent. So that Roger Fry and Carrington are the two best English artists according to Derain. Clive Bell will have to change his tune. As for Picasso he thinks all English art just pretty and sentimental.' In spite of Gertler's ironical note she was flattered enough to pass it on to Lytton.

4   Marriage

Ralph Partridge came seriously into her life in 1919 though she had met him once or twice with me as we had been close friends at Oxford before the war. He had served with distinction in the war both in France and Italy. Keen-witted and intellectually curious, he was notably handsome, strong and virile, and in fact could hardly have presented a stronger

Carrington with Ralph Partridge, Watendlath, 1921

Lytton Strachey and Ralph Partridge at Llanthony Abbey, 1923

Carrington and Gerald Brenan, 1921

physical contrast to the languid and delicate Lytton Strachey. It was something of a shock therefore to Carrington's friends when she and the 'Major', as they dubbed him, fell in love. During the Easter Vacation in 1919 Ralph and I had planned a walking tour in Spain and Carrington insisted on going too. By the end of it she and Ralph were lovers and during his next year at Oxford he was a frequent visitor to Tidmarsh. Lytton, always susceptible to youth and vigour, became as attached to Ralph as to Carrington, so that when the next year Ralph moved in to form a *ménage à trois* it did not seriously disturb the tenor of their existence – either Lytton's studies of Queen Victoria or Carrington's painting.

There were nevertheless inherent difficulties in such an arrangement, the most important being that for Carrington the contentment and comfort of Lytton had priority. This was the situation which Ralph had to accept and if he did so willingly at first it was because he fully appreciated the company and conversation of the Bloomsbury circle. For a time he worked as an assistant to Leonard Woolf's infant Hogarth Press, but he was soon forming other temporary attachments in London, which seemed natural and excusable enough. It was unfortunate that before long he insisted on marriage with Carrington, a move long resisted by her as against her principles, but eventually abetted by Lytton himself to preserve the *status quo* and because he feared Carrington's becoming too dependent upon himself. So in May 1921 they were married. She wrote to Gerald Brenan: 'At 10 o'clock at St. Pancras's shrine I shall change my beloved name of Carrington to a less noble one of Partridge. You smile and say "How are the stiff-necked fallen! Where are her grand principles!" They are still here young man, locked in my Amazon breast. I will never change my maiden name I have kept so long rings a good song. To you I shall ever be Carrington and to myself.'

A more serious complication in Carrington's life arose later in the same year when she herself fell in love with Gerald Brenan. He had come back to England for a while and was asked to join the Tidmarsh party up in the Lakes where they had rented a farm house. Gerald had served in the same unit as Ralph in France and they had become close friends. Determined to be independent of his family – Anglo-Indian and army – and to be a writer, he had settled in a remote mountain village in Andalusia. For a young man to sacrifice comfort and security for art of any kind was an action to command Carrington's interest. It was how she would have all her friends live. Neither she nor Gerald believed in exclusive relationships between men and women, but when the odd man out was a best friend, feelings of guilt were inevitably involved and these led to deceptions. There were crises once again which threatened to crack the harmony so recently established and it was re-established again only by the tact and persuasive power of Lytton himself, anxious that his home and family at Tidmarsh should not be wrecked.

Ham Spray House letterheadings, winter and summer versions, 1929

Naturally such affairs made more demands than ever on Carrington's time and powers of concentration, but for a while Gerald Brenan's interest in painting provided a fresh stimulus and some of her best work dates from these years. This can be seen not only in the pictures (Plates 12, 13 and 15) but in her letters. Of a Spanish landscape she wrote to him: 'I feel my picture is going to be one of the most beautiful in the world – is it partly because you blessed it with that magic one night?'

5 Ham Spray

In 1924 it was decided to look for another home. Tidmarsh had seemed an idyllic discovery – indeed life there at first

Carrington with her cat, Tiber, Ham Spray, 1929

seemed comparable with William Morris's Kelmscott further up the valley of the Thames as Morris describes it in his early letters. But the Mill House proved too damp and cold in winter and Lytton was often laid up for weeks, involving Carrington in more nursing than painting. With Ralph to drive the car that Lytton had now invested in, they discovered a farmhouse about twenty miles further west. It lay facing her beloved Hampshire downs, though it was just over the Wiltshire border near the village of Ham. Ham Spray was a square Regency house which had been added on to an older flint and brick farm. It was approached by an avenue of trees and had its own large walled garden ensuring privacy. Its great scenic attraction was the range of downs to the south, reached by a walk across a couple of open fields.

By this time Lytton found himself flush with royalties coming in from his *Queen Victoria* and he was able to purchase the house outright. Carrington and Ralph were in Spain and a telegram announcing the glad news brought them racing back. Carrington threw herself into the task of planning and decorating what she intended to be the most perfect home, where Lytton could write more masterpieces. She translated into paint her accumulated sketches so that their friends could be entertained in fitting surroundings. This then may be the place to say something of her decorative work which was an important side of her creative life. When still at the Slade she had joined one of the groups which from time to time did mural decorations in churches or village halls, and in the years before the war she was recruited by Roger Fry into the band of enthusiastic artists painting furniture or pottery at his Omega Workshops. Thereafter she undertook many commissions to decorate doors, panels or even gramophones for friends. In this she was undoubtedly influenced by Duncan Grant's work at Charleston. On a smaller scale she cut woodblocks as name plates for libraries and took a few commissions for the newly-founded Hogarth Press. A school edition of *Don Quixote*, which I had edited for the Oxford Press in India, was illustrated by her after one of her Spanish journeys and she would have willingly been engaged on more book illustration had it not at that time been subject to rather rigid conventions. While at Tidmarsh she painted several inn signs for local brewers. Of one of them she wrote to me: 'I guess it will be the only picture I shall ever get hung and seen by hundreds of people, not to mention horses and dogs.' Another of her more splendid signs was done for the Spread Eagle at Thame, which had been taken by the artist John Fothergill. He was perhaps the earliest of gentlemen-innkeepers who set out to revive the traditions of hostelries.

At Ham Spray she worked on several other crafts: bookbinding with patterned papers, glass pictures and decorated tiles. In the first of these crafts she had to give place to Ralph Partridge who, after studying at the Central School in London, had set himself up with a professional plant. Her glass paintings, using tinsel as a background, as well as paint, were a revival of a Victorian craft which she developed on her own individual lines. They were given to friends for the most part, but one London store took them up as a speciality. Tiles and plates she decorated on the 'biscuit', sending them to a pottery firm for glazing and firing. For these pieces there was a regular flow of commissions, but naturally few survived changes of ownership or removal. In the decoration of rooms she showed a natural gift and taste which was independent of the contemporary trends, that is to say either correct 'period' or ostentatiously functional. She chose furniture or textiles she liked from any period or country, and for Ham Spray Lytton delighted to surprise her with an Aubusson carpet, a four-poster bed or a botanical dictionary.

She was able to make Ham Spray her masterpiece both in its interior and in its garden; but it has to be admitted that the

Glass painting with tinsel, c.1926

41

flow of such commissions, whether to be executed at the homes of friends or in her studio, did compromise what she called her serious work, that is to say, painting. Originally they had been undertaken to earn the odd guinea or two, but there was no longer that need. And just as journalism becomes a distraction for writers who intend to write books, so her decorative crafts served as an excuse for putting off the getting down to bigger and more demanding tasks. The real truth went deeper than the demand on her time made by the commissions for craft work or even by entertaining or by parties in London. As she confided in her diary: 'This morning I felt those conflicting emotions were destroying my purpose in painting. It is perhaps that feeling which I have had ever since I came to London, years ago now, that I am not strong enough to live in this world of people *and* paint. It is a feeling which has complete truth in it.'

Dresser in the dining room at Ham Spray, 1926

6 Frustration

Thus in the later twenties Carrington's output of painting diminished. Too often the subject undertaken with enthusiasm was left unfinished, set aside to cope with the influx of visitors for the weekend. It had always been her prime consideration that Lytton should enjoy the company and conversation which his life at Cambridge and Bloomsbury had provided. Ham Spray was no great stately home: it was of comfortable farm-house size, with a large garden and a view of the Downs which could tempt the more energetic for walks. In addition to the carefully-selected guests a few friends from neighbouring counties could be invited. A good table was kept and wine imported in bulk was bottled in the capacious cellar. Two maids and a gardener formed the staff, but Carrington saw to it that the service was well maintained. The making of a country home had been the choice she had taken on herself and she never regarded it as a burden, but she was aware that her life as an artist increasingly suffered.

It had been of course a most delicately balanced system from its first inception; and some outsiders regarded it as absurd. Its extraordinary story has been recorded in detail by Michael Holroyd in his biography of Lytton Strachey and can be seen through Carrington's own eyes by readers of her letters. By 1928 the strains had become severe – more for her than the other two. Lytton was drawn away more and more often by his homosexual nature. Ralph Partridge had formed a more lasting attachment in London, though he remained closely involved in the Ham Spray menage. She had a wide circle of friends, both women and men, but there was no longer the secure rhythm of life that she needed as an artist. Her diary reveals too often long periods of ill-health, depression and morbid introspection, sleep disturbed by nightmares and remorse for her inability to return to the discipline of her

Tiled fireplace in Hampstead, 1930

Study for conversation piece at Ham Spray
House. Pen and ink drawing, c.1927

studio. A rather frantic love affair with a man younger than
herself brought more disillusion than joy. She was too honest
with herself to be able to hide the truth: 'I would like', she
writes in the last year of her life, 'this year, since for the first
time I seem to be without any relations to complicate me, to
do more painting. But then this is a resolution I have made for
years.'

In 1931 Lytton fell ill of an undiagnosed cancer and for
months fears and hopes alternated: Ham Spray filled with
nurses, relatives and anxious friends. When he was seen to be
dying she first attempted to take her life, but survived. She
agreed to give a trial to living without him but she never believed it possible. Lytton had meant everything to her that

made life worth living: 'I see my paints and think it is no use to me, for Lytton will not see it now.' And after returning from a visit to Biddesden, the home of her friends Brian and Diana Guinness, she wrote: 'The picture of the cook on the wall is perhaps one of the only pictures I ever brought off. I am glad that Lytton saw it and liked it.'

Her friends came to stop at Ham Spray to watch as well as to comfort and they tried to persuade her to come away to them; and the last to do so were Leonard and Virginia Woolf. But she preferred to stay alone at Ham Spray, going over her life with Lytton in the library she had designed for him or in the garden she had created for his enjoyment. Her last reference to her painting runs thus in her diary: 'Looked through all my old pictures to find some of Lytton to give to James [his brother]. Tidmarsh all came back. How much I love places. I remembered suddenly my passion for a certain tree in Burgess's back field. And the beauty of the mill at the back of the house and how once a kingfisher dived from the roof into the stream.'

Quoting from Sir Henry Wotton, 1627, she wrote:

> He first deceased. She for a little tried
> to live without him. Liked it not and died

and shortly before her thirty-ninth birthday she ended her life.

Note on the Paintings and Drawings

Owing to Carrington's reluctance to exhibit at galleries it has been difficult to make anything like a complete record of her work as an artist. During her lifetime she repainted many canvases, gave some to her friends and retained more in her home or studio at Ham Spray. On her death in 1932 her husband Ralph Partridge gave a number to myself and to friends, the rest remaining at Ham Spray where he settled after his second marriage and lived until his own death in 1960. His widow, Mrs Frances Partridge, then sold the house when the remaining pictures and drawings were distributed between her son and my own family.

The present volume contains more than half of Carrington's paintings that have so far been traced. Since the 1970 exhibition a few more pictures have come to light and it is hoped that this publication may reveal others. Some secondary studies of similar subjects have here been omitted for lack of space and a few because of their poor condition for reproduction. Amongst the drawings I have included some of her very early work as well as typical sketches intended for paintings. Her decorative work was usually commissioned for the homes of friends, and very little of this remains after fifty years. Most of her work can be dated from references in her letters or diaries.

THE PLATES

At a table nearby was sitting a young woman, I suppose of twenty-three or so, with short bobbed, pale yellow hair. This was Carrington, known by her surname, according to the Slade School custom, who was the first girl to wear her hair short. There was certainly an aura attaching to her, too, and one cannot but have every sympathy with the painter Mark Gertler, who loved her perhaps even at this time, and could not understand her devotion to the freakish and anything but kind-tongued Lytton Strachey. The two or three paintings that Carrington left behind her reveal her talent, and her personal touch shows in her letters. In her distinctive yet classless appearance she epitomised those few months and years of her own youth.

Sacheverell Sitwell: *For Want of a Golden City* (1973)

1 SAMUEL
   CARRINGTON:
   THE ARTIST'S
   FATHER
Oil painting
406 × 356 mm
(16in. × 14in.) 1915.
This was painted at
Hurstbourne a few
years before his death
in 1919 at the age of 87.
Carrington made many
drawings and several
paintings of him. *From
a private collection.*

2   RECLINING NUDE
Oil painting 508 × 762 mm (20in. × 30in.)
Prize-winning painting at the Slade
1912–13. *Reproduced by courtesy of the*
Slade School of Art, London.

3 HILLS IN SNOW AT
    HURSTBOURNE TARRANT
Watercolour 539 × 641 mm (21¼in. ×
25¼in.) 1916. This was painted at Hurstbourne, and is one of her few finished
watercolours. It was recently mistaken for
work by John Nash and Carrington was
probably influenced by him. She wrote to
Gertler at the time: 'Today it is snowing
white and a piercing wind. But I love the
hugeness of it and the great space between
one and the hills opposite.' *Reproduced by
courtesy of Mr Anthony Swiffen.*

4 GILES LYTTON STRACHEY
Oil painting 686 × 736 mm (27in. × 29in.)
1916. Painted in London. Studies for this painting are shown in Plate 35. Of the several paintings of Lytton she considered this the most successful. In her diary she wrote: 'Now tonight it looks wonderfully good, and I am happy. But then I dread showing it.' *From a private collection.*

5 THE MILL AT TIDMARSH,
   BERKSHIRE
Oil painting 711 × 1016 mm (28in. × 40in.)

1918. Painted at Tidmarsh. This is perhaps the most successful of the pictures she made of the mill, her home with Lytton from the end of 1917 to 1924. The black swans are an imaginative introduction. *From a private collection.*

6 LYTTON STRACHEY
   READING IN
   THE GARDEN AT
   TIDMARSH
Oil painting 730 × 533 mm
(28¾in. × 21in.) Painted probably
in 1918. *Reproduced by courtesy of
Mr and Mrs R. Strachey.*

54

7 LADY STRACHEY
Oil painting 762 × 609 mm
(30in. × 24in.) 1920. Painted
in London. It was one of her
few commissioned portraits,
for which she received £25.
She wrote to Lytton: 'This
morning I went to paint her
ladyship. She is superb. I
was completely overcome by
her grandeur and wit. I am
painting her against a
bookcase sitting full length
in a chair in a wonderful
robe which goes into great
El Greco folds. She looks
like the Queen of China or
one of El Greco's
Inquisitors.' *Reproduced by
courtesy of the Scottish
National Portrait Gallery,
Edinburgh.*

55

8 MRS BOX, FARMER'S WIFE AT
   WELCOMBE, CORNWALL
Oil painting 914 × 762 mm (36in. × 30in.)

1919. Between 1916 and 1919 Carrington
spent several holidays on the north coast of
Devon and Cornwall. Mrs Box, a real

country character, farming actively at 72,
became a great favourite of Carrington.
From a private collection.

9 FARM AT WATENDLATH
Oil painting 609 × 686 mm (24in. × 27in.)
1921. 'I sat and drew a white cottage and a barn . . . sitting on a little hill until it grew too cold . . . The trees are so marvellously solid, like trees in some old Titian pictures, and the houses such wonderful greys and whites, and then the formation of the hills so varied.' *From a private collection.*

10 GERALD BRENAN AT THE AGE OF TWENTY-EIGHT
Oil painting
495 × 406 mm
(19½in. × 16in.) 1921.
Probably painted at
Watendlath,
Cumberland, during
his visit to the farm.
*Reproduced by courtesy
of Mr John Wolfers.*

58

11 E. M. FORSTER
Oil painting
508 × 406 mm
(20in. × 16in.) 1920.
Painted at Tidmarsh,
where Morgan Forster
was a frequent visitor.
Reproduced by courtesy
of the National Portrait
Gallery, London.

12 MOUNTAIN RANGES FROM YEGEN, ANDALUSIA

Oil painting 686 × 787 mm (27in. × 31in.) c.1924. Painted at Tidmarsh. She was deeply affected by the Spanish landscape and made many studies during her two or three visits, working them up into paintings on her return. She wrote to Brenan: 'I am very happy working on two Yegen pictures. They transport me into another world. I cannot express quite the relief it is.' And later: 'I am working on the landscape you liked; the round mountains near the gorges. I am trying a new plan, an entire under-painting in brilliant colours, over which I shall glaze green and more transparent colours.' *From a private collection.*

13 HILL TOWN IN ANDALUSIA
Oil painting 317 × 406 mm (12½in. × 16in.)
c.1920. A village near Gerald Brenan's
home. *Reproduced by courtesy of Mr John
Wolfers. Photograph copyright Angelo
Hornak.*

14 THE RIVER PANG
   ABOVE TIDMARSH
Oil painting 762 × 635 mm
(30in. × 25in.) 1918. Painted
at Tidmarsh. She frequently
writes almost lyrically of this
scene, as to Gertler after her
first Christmas there: 'There
are wonderful Cézanne views
from the garden of the river
and trees.' *From a private
collection.*

15 BOY WITH
   CONCERTINA
Oil painting 635 × 508 mm
(25in. × 20in.) c.1924. It is
believed this was painted in
Spain at Gerald Brenan's
home in Andalusia. *From a
private collection.*

64

facing page
16   DAHLIAS
Oil painting (unfinished) 609 × 508 mm (24in. ×
20in.) c. 1927. Painted at Ham Spray. At this time
she was particularly interested in horticulture and
acquired a large collection of botanical prints.
From a private collection.

17   FAIRGROUND AT HENLEY
     REGATTA
Watercolour 330 × 432 mm (13in. × 17in.)
c.1920. Probably a design for a decorative
panel. Both Ralph Partridge and her brother
rowed at Henley. *From a private collection.*

**18 TIDMARSH MILL AND
      MEADOWS**
Oil painting 686 × 686 mm (27in. × 27in.)

c.1920. Painted at Tidmarsh. She wrote a
few days before her death: 'Tidmarsh all
came back . . . and the beauty of the mill at
the back of the house and how once a
kingfisher dived from the roof into the
stream.' *From a private collection*.

66

19 FISHING BOATS IN THE
    MEDITERRANEAN
Oil painting 356 × 330 mm (14in. × 13in.)

c.1923. A watercolour sketch of the same
scene is in existence. *From a private
collection.*

20 LYTTON STRACHEY IN HIS
   LIBRARY
Oil painting 711 × 533 mm (28in. × 21in.)
c.1922. Painted at Tidmarsh. The original
of this portrait was given by the artist after
Lytton's death to his brother James. The
drawing for it is illustrated above right.
*Reproduced by courtesy of Mr Anthony
d'Offay.*

facing page
21 JULIA STRACHEY
Oil painting 381 × 330 mm (15in. × 13in.)
1928. Julia was the daughter of Oliver and
niece of Lytton. She married Stephen
Tomlin, the sculptor, and after his death
Lawrence Gowing, author and art critic.
She has written several novels. *Reproduced
by courtesy of Mr and Mrs R. Strachey.*

**22 CATHARINE
      CARRINGTON**
Oil painting 406 × 305 mm
(16in. × 12in.) 1926. Painted at
Ham Spray. She was the artist's
sister-in-law. *From a private
collection.*

facing page
23 ANNIE
Oil painting 508 × 406 mm
(20in. × 16in.) c.1917. Painted at
Tidmarsh. Annie was the good-
natured maid-of-all-work at
Tidmarsh and subsequently for
a time at Ham Spray.
From a private collection.

24 CIRCUS HORSES   Oil painting on wood panel 330 × 736 mm (13in. × 29in.) c.1927. Possibly intended for a decoration. *Reproduced by courtesy of Mr G. Heywood Hill.*

25 CHILDREN WITH NUNS
ON BEACH
Oil painting 324 × 362 mm (12¾in. × 14¼in.)

c.1927. Probably painted in Normandy. Though there is no mention in letters of this work Carrington probably painted it on a visit to her friend Phyllis de Tanze. *Reproduced by courtesy of Mrs Henrietta Partridge.*

26 JANIE BUSSY.
Oil painting 609 × 838 mm (24in. × 33in.)
c.1928. Painted at Ham Spray. Janie Bussy
was the daughter of Simon Bussy, the
French artist, and Lytton Strachey's sister
Dorothy. She was a frequent guest at Ham
Spray. *Reproduced by courtesy of Mrs
Barbara Bagenal.*

27 THE DOWNS FROM HAM
      SPRAY IN WINTER
Oil painting 305 × 356 mm (12in. × 14in.).
Painted during the winter of 1929–30.
From a private collection.

facing page
28 CATTLE BY A POND
Oil painting 406 × 356 mm (16in. × 14in.)
c.1930. Painted at Ham Spray. The downs
may be seen in the background. *From a
private collection.*

facing page
29 THE DOWNS FROM
 HAM SPRAY
Unfinished oil painting 660 × 610 mm
(26in. × 24in.) c.1928. Few pictures of this
late period survive, but there are references
on several occasions to the start of a subject
like this. *Reproduced by courtesy of Mrs
Julia Gowing.*

30 SELF PORTRAIT
Pencil drawing 228 × 152 mm (9in. × 6in.)
c.1910. The hair style confirms that this
was drawn not later than her first year at
the Slade. *From a private collection.*

31 STUDIES OF HER
FATHER AND SECOND
BROTHER
Pencil drawings 330 × 254 mm
(13in. × 10in.) 1911. Her father was
the subject of many studies of this
type as well as being posed
for compositions. *From a private
collection.*

facing page
32 PORTRAIT OF HER
BROTHER NOEL
Pencil drawing 305 × 254 mm
(12in. × 10in.) c.1910. At this time
her brother, two years younger
than herself, was still at school.
From a private collection.

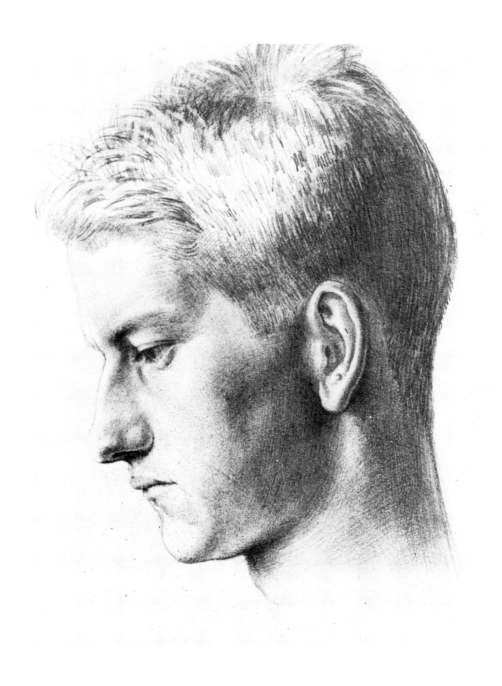

33 PORTRAIT OF HER BROTHER TEDDY
Pencil drawing 254 × 190 mm (10 in. × 7½ in.) c. 1912. Made while he was still at Cambridge. During the war he served on a minesweeper and was known as her 'sailor brother'. He later transferred to the Army and was killed on the Somme in 1916. *From a private collection.*

34 SLADE STUDENT IN FANCY
   DRESS
Watercolour and pencil drawing 552 × 298
mm (21¾in. × 11¾in.) Signed and dated
1913. Regarded as self portrait. *Reproduced
by courtesy of the Mercury Gallery, London.*

83

35 STUDIES FOR
PORTRAIT OF
LYTTON
STRACHEY
Pencil drawings
356 × 254 mm (14in. × 10in.)
1916. For the oil portrait,
Plate 4. *From a private
collection.*

above
36 LYTTON STRACHEY AND
      BORIS ANREP
Pen and ink drawing 356 × 330 mm
(14in. × 13in.) c.1927. Made at Ham Spray,
probably as a study for a painting. *Reproduced by courtesy of Mr Charles Whaley.*

below
    A GAME OF CHESS AT
    HAM SPRAY
Pen and ink drawing 197 × 254 mm
(7¾in. × 10in.) c.1926. *Reproduced by
courtesy of the Harvane Gallery, London.*

85

37 LYTTON STRACHEY READING
Pen and wash drawing, dimensions un-
known, c.1920. Original lost. Made at
Tidmarsh.

86

38 RECLINING NUDE
Pencil and wash drawing 228 × 356 mm
(9in. × 14in.). Probably a late drawing.
From a private collection.

39 LYTTON STRACHEY'S LIBRARY
   AT HAM SPRAY
Designed by Carrington. Photograph
taken c.1926.

Select Bibliography

The following works are of interest either because they mention Carrington directly or because they are concerned with people with whom she was closely connected.
Place of publication is London unless otherwise indicated.

BEDFORD, SYBILLE. *Aldous Huxley*. Collins, 1973.

BELL, CLIVE. *Old Friends: Personal Recollections*. Chatto and Windus, 1956.

BELL, QUENTIN. *Bloomsbury*. Weidenfeld and Nicolson, 1968.

BELL, QUENTIN. *Virginia Woolf*. Hogarth Press, 1972.

BRENAN, GERALD. *South from Granada*. Hamish Hamilton, 1957.

BRENAN, GERALD. *A Life of One's Own*. Hamish Hamilton, 1962.

BRENAN, GERALD. *A Personal Record*. Jonathan Cape, 1974.

BURNS, EDWARD (ed.). *Letters of Alice B. Toklas*. Angus and Robertson, 1974.

CANNAN, GILBERT. *Mendel: A Story of Youth*. Fisher Unwin, 1916.

CARRINGTON, NOEL (ed.). *Selected Letters of Mark Gertler*. Hart-Davis, 1965.

DARROCH, SANDRA. *Ottoline*. Chatto and Windus, 1976.

DEVAS, NICOLETTE. *Two Flamboyant Fathers*. Collins, 1966.

GADD, DAVID. *The Loving Friends*. Hogarth Press, 1974.

GARNETT, DAVID. *Flowers of the Forest*. Chatto and Windus, 1955.

GARNETT, DAVID. *The Familiar Faces*. Chatto and Windus, 1962.

GARNETT, DAVID. *The Golden Echo*. Chatto and Windus, 1970.

GARNETT, DAVID (ed.). *Carrington : Letters and Extracts from her Diaries*. Jonathan Cape, 1970. Paperback O.U.P., 1979.

GLENAVY, LADY BEATRICE. *Today We Will Only Gossip*. Constable, 1964.

HARDY, ROBERT GATHORNE (ed.). *The Early Memoirs of Lady Ottoline Morrell*. Faber, 1963.

HARDY, ROBERT GATHORNE (ed.). *Ottoline of Garsington*. Faber, 1974.

HOLROYD, MICHAEL. *Lytton Strachey*. Heinemann, 1968. Republished as *Lytton Strachey : A Biography* and *Lytton Strachey and the Bloomsbury Group : His Work, Their Influence*. Penguin, 1971.

HOLROYD, MICHAEL. *Lytton Strachey by Himself*. Heinemann, 1971.

HOLROYD, MICHAEL. *Augustus John*. Heinemann, 1974.

HUXLEY, ALDOUS. *Crome Yellow*. Chatto and Windus, 1921.

JOHNSTONE, J. K. *The Bloomsbury Group*. Secker and Warburg, 1954.

LEHMANN, JOHN. *Virginia Woolf and Her World*. Thames and Hudson, 1975.

LEVY, PAUL (ed.). *Lytton Strachey : The Really Interesting Question*. Weidenfeld and Nicolson, 1972.

MACCARTHY, SIR DESMOND. *Memories*. MacGibbon and Kee, 1953.

MOORE, HENRY J. (ed.). *Selected Letters of D. H. Lawrence*. Heinemann, 1962.

NICOLSON, NIGEL (ed.). *The Flight of the Mind : The Letters of Virginia Woolf*. Vol. I: 1888–1912. Hogarth Press, 1975.

NICOLSON, NIGEL (ed.). *The Question of Things Happening : The Letters of Virginia Woolf*. Vol. II: 1912–1922. Hogarth Press, 1976.

NOBLE, JOAN RUSSELL (ed.). *Recollections of Virginia Woolf*. Peter Owen, 1972.

ROTHENSTEIN, JOHN. *Modern English Painters*. Macdonald and Jane's, 1976.

SANDERS, CHARLES R. *The Strachey Family*. Duke University Press, Durham, North Carolina, 1953.

SANDERS, CHARLES R. *Lytton Strachey : His Mind and Art*. Yale University Press, New Haven, Conn., 1957.

SHONE, RICHARD. *Bloomsbury Portraits*. Phaidon, 1976.

SMITH, GROVER (ed.). *The Letters of Aldous Huxley*. Chatto and Windus, 1969.

STRACHEY, LYTTON. *Eminent Victorians*. Chatto and Windus, 1918.

STRACHEY, LYTTON. *Queen Victoria*. Chatto and Windus, 1921.

STRACHEY, LYTTON. *Elizabeth and Essex*. Chatto and Windus, 1928.

SUTTON, DENYS (ed.). *The Letters of Roger Fry*. Chatto and Windus, 1972.

WATERS, GRANT M. *Dictionary of British Artists Working 1900–1950*. Eastbourne Fine Art, Eastbourne, 1975.

WOODESON, JOHN. *Mark Gertler : Biography of a Painter 1891–1939*. Sidgwick and Jackson, 1972.

WOOLF, LEONARD. *Downhill All the Way*. Hogarth Press, 1974.

WOOLF, LEONARD AND VIRGINIA. *Two Stories*. Hogarth Press, 1917. (With woodcuts by Carrington.)

WOOLF, VIRGINIA. *Roger Fry*. Hogarth Press, 1940.

Index